BREAK SUGAR CRAVINGS or ADDICTION, FEEL FULL, LOSE WEIGHT

An Astonishing Essential Oil Method

Part of the Sublime Wellness Lifestyle Series #3

By Kathy Heshelow
Amazon Best-Selling Author
Founder of Sublime Naturals®

GET A **FREE** THERAPEUTIC-GRADE PEPPERMINT ESSENTIAL OIL when you Buy a 50% Off THERAPEUTIC-GRADE GRAPEFRUIT ESSENTIAL OIL or ANY Other Essential Oil (with Free Shipping) + Safety Tips + My Next Book Free:

https://goo.gl/VNvdL3

These are important natural tools to help break sugar cravings, stop overeating and lose weight, which you will read about in this book.

PREFACE

I have a little story about the title of this book. I was wrestling with whether to start the title of the book with "Break Sugar Addiction" or "Stop Sugar Cravings". The fact is, many people don't realize that they actually are addicted to sugar (you will learn **WHY** in this book) and so I didn't want to scare people away or have those people not even consider the book. However, should I avoid the word addiction totally?

I decided to put the question to a great group of mastermind authors I belong to – and wow! I received such passionate stories and responses, for both approaches. Numerous authors told me that they had been addicted to sugar but didn't realize it until they had addressed health or weight issues, and dug in for themselves. A few have children who are allergic or sugar-sensitive. Many weighed in on cravings.

The group's opinion was evenly split over which approach to use, which told me what I needed to know. I decided to use both words, "Break Sugar Addiction or Cravings"...

I hope you do enjoy this book. At the very least, it can awaken you to some facts that are not commonly known. At the most, it could end up improving your health and wellness!

~ Kathy Heshelow

Table of Contents

WHO IS THIS BOOK FOR?

This book was written for anyone interested in their health and wellness, and who want to know more about what they put into their bodies.

It is **especially meant** for those who find they have sugar cravings; for those who are overweight and are trying to lose weight; and those who eat even when they are full. It can definitely help those who find they can't stop eating sweets. The natural method discussed is one to help get the situation under control - naturally.

I reveal some interesting and shocking facts about sugar, and cite research from experts in the field which are evidence-based. I give you the WHYS and the HOWS on the subject.

I do not advocate or lay out any type of diet in this book. In fact, I personally think most "diets" are doomed to fail because of the "deprivation mindset", and that we should approach eating in a balanced way right for our body types and needs. This includes avoiding additives, preservatives and unnatural foods.

Did you know that *"...95% of people who lose weight by dieting will regain it in 1-5 years,"* says a Psychology Today article. *"Since dieting, by definition, is a* temporary food plan, *so it won't work in the long run. Moreover, the deprivation of restrictive diets may lead to a diet-overeat or diet-binge cycle."* (1)

This is why I do believe in breaking free of any sugar addiction, taking back satiety control and then finding foods and appropriate portions that work for you and your overall lifestyle. I talk a bit about this in the last chapter.

The purpose of this book is to reveal HOW you can address the issue of sugar addiction and over-eating, break it, find a healthier path for your body - **and to give you the tools for success.** You will learn that your brain is key to the problem, and the tools go right to the source to help you.

I also wrote this book because <u>far too many people do NOT know what is in their food, or the harm it could be doing</u> (or IS doing) to their bodies and long-term health.

Some take action to lose weight, but might use medications that could do harm, or use approaches that fail because they don't get to the source of the problem, or overlook the impact of the brain and natural body reactions (and those sugar cravings that could ruin it all.)

The method proposed in this book is fully natural, and goes to the source to help you make changes in your life, your relationship with food or sugar, your addictions or cravings – and get you on the right path.

Remember this: You are ultimately in control and decision-making of what you put into your body, how you nourish it and how you care for your health. I simply want to help you on a path to improved wellness (it's what the Sublime Wellness Lifestyle Series is all about!)

Even for those not grappling with weight problems or sugar cravings, I wrote this book because far too many people do NOT know what is in their food, or the harm it could be doing (or IS doing) to their bodies and long-term health.

As a final note, I lived in Paris, France for 16 years and can tell you that the French DO NOT do diets. They are true gourmands, enjoy food as a great pleasure and even as an art – and yet you rarely see overweight French people. They don't understand why Americans always seem to be on diets, depriving themselves of a basic pleasure, yet so many are overweight. They have a healthy relationship with food, and by the way, they consume FAR less sugar (despite those lovely bakeries) and food with far less additives than us. You will learn a little about this in the book.

CHAPTER 1
ASTONISHING AND LITTLE KNOWN FACTS ABOUT SUGAR

Let's start this journey with a number of facts. I have written this chapter as number of bullet points, drawn from many sources. The purpose is to break down startling facts that are easy to understand and "consume", one by one, and to build a body of facts that should speak for themselves.

SUGAR FACTS

Did you know this? Sugar reacts with and induces a response in the same part of your brain as cocaine, heroin and nicotine. It stimulates the release of dopamine neuro-transmitters in a kind of "high" or "rush" of addictive pleasure. This fact is KEY as to why you get cravings, why you may be addicted, and why our method can work.

- "We now eat in two weeks the amount of sugar that our ancestors of 200 years ago ate in a whole year," said University of London nutritionist John Yudkin said of the British and Americans in 1963 (1)

- Just look at how sugar consumption has increased over time. (2)
    In 1700, the average person consumed about 4 pounds of sugar per year.

In 1800, the average person consumed about 18 pounds of sugar per year.

In 1900, individual consumption had risen to 90 pounds of sugar per year.

In 2009, more than 50 percent of all Americans consume <u>one-half pound of sugar PER DAY</u>—translating to a <u>whopping 180 pounds of sugar per year</u>!

- A South African research paper concluded that humans **could <u>"tolerate"</u> as much as 70 pounds per year** of sugar (what Americans and Brits were consuming in the 1870s) before diabetes would develop. (3) X the case for sugar

- Today **1 in 11 of every American has diabetes.**

- In the U.S. **through the mid-nineteenth century, <u>diabetes was a rare disease</u>!** But in 2012, more than 2 million Americans were diagnosed (a case every 16 seconds), mainly Type 2 (associated with obesity).

- The greatest surge so far of diabetes in the U.S. has been from 1960 to the present, with an 800% increase which coincides with a significant rise in the consumption of sugar and sweeteners (including the deadly high fructose corn syrup). A study mentioned later in this chapter shows that **consumption of high fructose corn syrup increased 1000%** since 1970, <u>more than any other food, drink or food group during the same time period, mirroring the gross rise</u> in obesity and diabetes.

- Diabetics will have a higher possibility of stroke, heart disease, liver and kidney disease, oral disease, failing eyesight and more. **The pharmaceutical market for diabetes drugs is more than $30 billion dollars per year, for a disease that was rare and almost non-existent a century ago**, before the rise of sugar consumption. A new report forecasts $55 billion for diabetes drugs by the end of 2017. (4)

- Sugar: there are no nutrients, no proteins, no essential fats, no vitamins or minerals in sugar... it's just "empty" calories.

- In fact, **when natural sugar is refined, 64 important nutrients or elements of sugar are destroyed**. That is, all of its vitamins (A, B and D) are wiped out along with the calcium, potassium, magnesium, iron, manganese, phosphate, and sulfate. Even its enzymes and fiber and fats are taken out. It's just empty and fully "refined".

- What's worse, **ingesting sugar actually can cause your body to deplete its own stores** of various vitamins, minerals and enzymes because of this refinement! More minerals are needed from your body to correct the imbalance, which can then cause osteoporosis and other problems. Plus this process damages cells and plays a role in aging, or aging faster. It becomes a "monster within."

- "The average healthy digestive system can digest and eliminate from two to four teaspoons of sugar daily, usually without noticeable problems (that is if damage is not already present). But, **just one 12 oz. Coca Cola contains 11 (eleven) teaspoons of sugar**... It is easy to see why America's health is in serious trouble." (5)

- Experts call sugar the worst "food" of all. In fact, Dr. David Reuben, author of "Everything You Always Wanted to Know About Nutrition" says, "...white refined sugar is not a food. It is a pure chemical extracted from plant sources, purer in fact than cocaine, which it resembles in many ways." (6)

- Yet, the single largest source of calories in our diet as Americans comes from sugar, and even worse, the highest percentage of this is from high fructose corn syrup (HFCS).

- There are 2 extremely bad things about processed fructose. 1] HFCS **turns off your appetite-control and satiety controls**, and 2] processed HFCS is **metabolized entirely in your liver** (instead of the "normal" way like glucose, without burden to your liver.) HFCS is behind the growing problem of liver disorders and fatty liver.

- A paper published in The American Journal of Clinical Nutrition lays blame on high fructose corn syrup (HFCS) for the epidemic of obesity. The paper, entitled "Consumption of High-Fructose Corn Syrup in Beverages May Play a Role in the Epidemic of Obesity" by George A Bray, Samara Joy Nielsen, and Barry M Popkin. Food consumption patterns were analyzed with U.S. Department of Agriculture tables from 1967 to 2000. The consumption of HFCS increased more than 1000% between 1970 and 1990, far exceeding the changes in intake of any other food or food group. HFCS represents more than 40% of caloric sweeteners added to foods and beverages - and is the sole sweetener in soft drinks. The increased use of HFCS in the United States mirrors the rapid increase in obesity. (7)

- Today **1 in every 10 adolescents has nonalcoholic fatty liver disease** and 75 million adults suffer. The link? Fructose is metabolized in the liver AND is fat producing. It's become an epidemic.

- Fructose elevates your uric acid levels, which in turn raises blood pressure and hurts the kidneys, and can cause faster weight gain.

- "…The vital organs in the body are actually damaged by this gross intake of sugar." (8)

- As Gary Taubes says in "The Case Against Sugar", a third of all American adults are obese, two-thirds are overweight, one in seven is diabetic and one in four or five will die of cancer. But 50 years ago, only one in eight was obese… rates have dramatically increased. What has changed? One dramatic increase is the intake of sugar. (9)

- Diabetes has seriously grown, as we have seen. **There is now a growing link between Alzheimer's and Type 2 Diabetes.** These observations began in the mid 1990's. Studies have been done in Japan, Holland and the U.S. and continue. Type 2 Diabetes patients have 1 ½ to 2 times the risk of developing Alzheimer's. Researchers have suggested numerous possibilities but blood sugar and inflammation are at the top of the list. Insulin resistance can go awry in the brain. Some researchers now even refer to Alzheimer's as Type 3 Diabetes.

- **Sugar is being linked to potential confusion in the brain and mental issues, such as Alzheimer's disease.** Our brains are very sensitive and react to chemical changes within the body. As sugar is consumed, our cells are robbed of their B vitamin, which destroys them, and insulin production is inhibited. Low insulin production means a high sugar (glucose) level in the bloodstream, which can lead to a confused mental state or unsound mind.

- There is also a growing link to **Parkinson's disease**, as those who suffer from this disease may have a higher sugar intake.

- **There is a definite link between cancer and sugar.** Cancer is one of the leading causes of death worldwide and is characterized by **uncontrolled growth and multiplication of cells. Insulin is one of the key hormones in regulating this sort of growth.** For this reason, many scientists believe that having constantly elevated insulin levels (a consequence of sugar consumption) can contribute to cancer. (10)

- In fact, whatever causes the insulin resistance could be promoting the transformation of healthy cells into malignant metastatic cells by increasing insulin secretion, elevating blood sugar and telling the cells to take up increasing more glucose for fuel." (11)

- The esteemed Sayer Ji says, "**Cancer cells prefer to ferment sugar as a form of energy** even when there is sufficient oxygen available to the cells to do so; hence Warburg's description of cancer metabolism as 'aerobic glycolysis' or the so-called 'Warburg effect'." (12)

- **With too much sugar, an acidic imbalance can occur in the body.** When our pH is balanced between acidic and alkaline, the body is healthy. Most disease states can't exist when the body's pH is alkaline or balanced – but they can and do in an acidic body. Bacteria, viruses and fungi like the acid environment. So what's a body pumped full of sugar an environment for?

- **Sugar makes the blood very thick and sticky**, and this can impair circulation in smaller capillaries.

- Sugar can often lead drowsiness, loss of focus and crankiness.

- It can bring on headaches, dizziness, promotes chronic degenerative diseases, agitates intestinal issues and contributes to auto-immune diseases.

- **Inflammation.** Inflammation is behind many problems and diseases. It's a relatively newly understood issue. Dr. Dave Grotto says in the book Sugar Crush by Dr. Richard Jacoby, "Sugar can play a role in inflammatory diseases. Poor regulation of glucose and insulin is a breeding ground for inflammation." (13)

- Chronic inflammation is implicated in a range of conditions from IBS, allergies, arthritis and rheumatoid arthritis to heart and disease. It damages the immune system, raises blood pressure, inflames blood vessels and much more.

- **Sugar is definitely detrimental to our oral health**. It damages teeth and causes cavities. Sugar creates an environment for bad bacteria and cavities to develop, gum disease and the plethora of oral issues. Oral health is linked to overall wellness of the body, and has a direct correlation to heart, lung and kidney disease.

- **The Surgeon General reports that at least 80% of American adults have gum disease**. Gum Disease increases the risk for heart disease, high blood pressure and even stroke. The high level of gum disease may be linked to the high level of sugar in our diet.

You see, sugar (and sugar addiction) is one of the most deadly of addictions. Because sugar seems so innocent and sweet (no pun intended), so easy to obtain and available at every turn (whether we want it or not, hidden in many foods), it is a serious threat.

HOW DID WE GET HERE?

- Sugar has been used in various forms throughout history, cited in ancient Egypt and in ancient cultures. It only started to appear in Europe when Crusaders returned in the 11th century. It was regarded as quite precious and was expensive – but was only typically available a few months per year. Columbus brought sugar to the new world in 1493, starting sugarcane plantations in the Caribbean. However, it remained an expensive commodity like oil of today. It wasn't until the 1800s that sugar refineries started to proliferate, and many New York families were made wealthy from it – and the U.S. government! In the 1880s, more than half a billion dollars had been collected in sugar taxes, reported in the New York Times of the day.

- Sugar, its production and availability, changed with the industrial revolution. Sugar refineries could now produce millions of pounds of sugar per day in 1920, as much as it would have produced in an entire DECADE in the 1820s (14) This helped make it cheap and more accessible.

- Sugar was transformed from a "luxury of kings into a kingly luxury of commoners" (as Sidney Mintz has described), first in the U.K and then in the U.S. as it became cheaper and easier to produce. (15)

- The modern U.S. candy industry launched in Boston in 1847, first using hand-cranked machines, then horse-powered, then steam-powered and finally electic-powered, changing from a niche industry of sweets for the rich to sweets for all. By 1903, it was estimated that the annual industry was at $150 million from almost nothing 25 years earlier.

- Soft drinks or sodas also were "invented" in the late 1880s and by the early 1900's, sales were increasing tenfold each year.

- Sugar content in cigarettes (many don't know this) was an American invention at about the same time, in the early 1900's with the American blended cigarettes. A certain tobacco leaf that was dried to be used in blends ends up containing as much as 22% sugar, helping to make the acidic smoke easier to inhale (and even more addictive.)

- **Candy, sweets and ice cream consumption doubled with the beginning of Prohibition in 1919.** Americans were denied one "vice" and replaced it with another. In fact, a number of breweries were converted to candy factories during Prohibition.

- **Sugar is now everywhere in the food industry.** Did you know that sugar is not just in the obvious, like candy, cookies, ice cream, sodas, jams & jellies, and cereals but also in the less obvious like lunch meats, peanut butter, pretzels, chips, spaghetti sauces, canned soups, dressings, ketchup, meats and more. Sugar is used as a preservative as well as sweetener.

- **Sugar was added to flour to help the yeast to rise**, to preserve and to make it "more tasty". Throughout the 20th century, sugar content has risen steadily in U.S. breads, feeding our "sweet tooth" syndrome. Wonder Bread, for instance, can have more than 10% sugar while a Parisian bread will have 2%.

- **In rare occasions when sugar consumption declined since the 1900's (such as during World War I due to rationing), diabetes mortality declined too.** (16)

- **"The food industry has made it [sugar] into a diet staple because they know when they do, you buy more. This is their hook.** If some unscrupulous cereal manufacturer went out and laced your breakfast cereal with morphine to get you to buy more, what would you think of that? They do it with sugar instead," says Dr. Robert Lustig in The Guardian. (His book is "Fat Chance: The Bitter Truth About Sugar".) (17)

- As Robert Lustig says in his book, "Fat Chance: Beating the Odds Against Sugar, Processed Food, Obesity and Disease", in the 1970s, the U.S. government declared that we needed to get the fat our of our diets. The food industry responded by replacing the fat with sugar and by removing fiber to extend its product shelf lives.

- Since the 1980s, when fats in foods were commonly thought to be the main cause of obesity, food manufacturers advertise their goods as "healthy" **if they were low in fat but replaced those calories with sugar** (fructose-glucose combinations and high-fructose corn syrup.) So, fat was taken out of candy, yogurts and other goods, but <u>sugar was added</u> and many are advertised as "heart healthy" or "low fat healthy".

- **Fats in food as the culprit for obesity lost out to sugar for a century, and let the sugar industry grow without serious medical-circle concerns.** A dominant theory in our generation was that fat in foods were bad and caused obesity, not sugar. However, researchers began to notice various facts and trends. One was that the French, with a diet rich in saturated fats, were not obese and had low heart disease. It had been ignored that the French consumed far less sugar than Americans or Brits (despite all those patisseries!). In the 18th century, the French per capita sugar consumption was less than a fifth of the UK. By the end of the 19th century, France was still far behind at 33 pounds vs. 88 for the Brits and 66 for Americans. Today it is still far less.

- In France, people consume about **5 tablespoons of sugar per day while in the U.S. people consume 11 tablespoons per day!** While my friends in France say it is starting to change, it is still rare to see an obese Frenchmen (I didn't notice any last year on our trip there, and it was rare in my 16 years living there to see it) – this in the land of the gourmand and rich foods.

- Let's also highlight the fact that high fructose corn syrup **(HFCS) is used heavily in the U.S. and Canada, <u>but sparingly or not at all in Japan and most of Europe</u>.**

- Fructose and HFCS activates a liver enzyme, which is a bridge between liver metabolism and inflammation, says Dr. Lustig, which leads to liver insulin resistance and can lead eventually to diabetes.

- Dr. Richard Jacoby writes, in his book "Sugar Crush" about the importance of some fat in the diet: "This is an extremely important point, but most of my patients don't get it. Many of <u>my patients don't understand that their weight problems and illnesses are caused not by the fat in their diets but by the massive amounts of sugar and unrefined carbs </u>they eat. They've been told for so long that far is bad that they simply take it for granted as true." (18)

- **Dr. Mercola's new book, "<u>Fat for Fuel</u>", will be released after this book, but his main theme follows this very point –** that fat is an important fuel for the body. He says that we can be far more successful at losing weight when we burn fat for fuel instead of carbs – and by shifting over to a state of nutritional ketosis where your body uses fat as its primary energy source, cravings for sugar and junk foods will go down.

- Thankfully, today there has been a shift of understanding about sugar consumption, triglycerides in the blood, diabetes and heart disease. The medical researchers started to recognize insulin resistance and a condition called "**metabolic syndrome**" was the major risk factor for heart disease and diabetes (not fats).

- **Metabolic syndrome** is basically a disruption to the body and insulin resistance causing any number of conditions, like obesity, high blood pressure, heart disease, high trigycerides in the blood, inflammation, liver disease. **The source of problem – overconsumption of sugar** though some researchers cited carbs, too.

- Metabolic syndrome is classically defined as a cluster of five chronic conditions – obesity, diabetes, lipid problems, high blood pressure and cardiovascular disease.

- It's a vicious cycle: secreting too much insulin can cause insulin resistance, and insulin resistance will cause the body to secrete more insulin.

What causes insulin resistance? There has not been rigorous testing on this, but most assume it is sedentary lifestyle and little exercise with poor diet high in sugars and excess fat accumulation.

ADDICTION

So can you really get addicted to sugar? Read on.

- When you ingest sugar, there is a massive dopamine release, and this is indeed addictive. Like abusive drugs, sugar causes a release of dopamine creates a "high" in the reward center of the brain, the Nucleus Accumbens. (19)

- Those who are more susceptible to addiction can become strongly addicted to sugar and sugary foods. But everyone is at risk.

- In other words, the same center in the brain that fires up with crack and heroin is affected with sugar.

- Did you ever see the "Star Trek: Next Generation" episode called The Game? Ryker brings a game back to the Enterprise, given to him by an evil woman. A headpiece is worn while the game is played. Each level of the game fires up the pleasure center of the brain. More and more of the crew are getting addicted, with the intention of the evil race to control and take over the Enterprise. Sugar is like this.

- When you get the "pleasure hit" of sugar, you want more and eat more to get the rush, and you repeat the behavior. As you repeat that behavior of eating more sugar, your brain adjusts to release less dopamine. The only way to feel the same "high" as before is to repeat the behavior in increasing amounts and frequency. This is known as substance abuse and addiction. And this clearly happens with sugar.

"Research shows that sugar can be even more addicting than cocaine," says Cassie Bjork, R.D., L.D., founder of Healthy Simple Life. "Sugar activates the opiate receptors in our brain and affects the reward center, which leads to compulsive behavior, despite the negative consequences like weight gain, headaches, hormone imbalances, and more....Studies suggest that every time we eat sweets we are reinforcing those neuropathways, **causing the brain to become increasingly hardwired to crave sugar...**" she adds. ([20](20))

- Did you know that doctors and various clinical studies have suggested that weaning an alcoholic or drug-abuser with sugar - sugary drinks - helps to transfer one addiction to another. Neurologist James Leonard Corning said, "There is little doubt that sugar can allay the physical cravings of alcohol." (21) But what about sugar addiction and health problems this creates?

- We are being fed sugar directly and indirectly, and it is consuming us. No wonder we are addicted. The issue is that most of us don't even know it. It's a national disaster.

- Dr. Alan Greene says, "I'm serious when I say that evidence is mounting that too much sugar could lead to true addiction." (22)

SHOCKING TEST BUT A HOPEFUL RESULT

Since the 1990s researchers established that if you feed animals pure fructose or sugar (glucose-fructose), their livers convert the sugar to fat, the same condition that gives us heart disease. Continue to feed them this in high amounts, and the fat accumulates in the liver and insulin resistance forms, resulting in metabolic syndrome and diabetes.

It can develop in a week if animals are given 70% of their diet in sugar, and in several months if the percentage (20%) is closer to what Americans consume.

Here is the hopeful part: **WHEN THEY STOPPED FEEDING THE ANIMALS SUGAR, THE FATTY LIVER WENT AWAY AND THE INSULIN RESISTANCE WENT AWAY.**

In another test with rhesus monkeys (in 2011), 29 monkeys were given the opportunity to drink a fructose-sweetened drink along with their usual food. They all drank, and every one of them developed insulin resistance and metabolic syndrome within the year, with 4 progressing to type 2 diabetes.

The correlation that many draw is that if sugar causes insulin resistance such as animal studies have shown, it is likely the trigger for excess fat accumulation and obesity. **When sugar is removed, insulin resistance improves, weight is lost.**

- **Why isn't this more known**? Cutting the sugar could help innumerable people. Too much sugar and fructose is everywhere, a serious basic problem of daily life. Take away the sugar (or excess sugar and fructose), and insulin resistance improves, weight is lost. Yes, other factors like the rest of the diet, how much exercise the person is getting, and how damaged his organs and overall health is at play. But nevertheless....

There are so many obese or overweight people, consuming hidden and unhidden sugar, gaining weight, feeding the addiction, developing diabetes and heart disease and liver problems, on medications, many deteriorating in health and craving the sugar. Some try to lose weight but can't do it – fructose turns off the satiety function and so they overeat and it also creates a desire for more. Depression can set in and for some, emotional eating then compounds the problem, and overall health deteriorates.

- As early as in 1978, a leading diabetes authority, Kelly West, said that diabetes had already killed more people in the 20th century than all wars combined. (23)

I contend that sugar and what it does to the body and wellness must be addressed and recognized by us all.

Those who are addicted, who are ill or obese, have an urgent reason to break the addiction and get on a good path. But every those who are not sick or diabetic need to understand what sugar is doing, that it is eating away at your wellness, and take measures to reduce or replace.

What about eating fruit?

"There's no need to avoid the naturally occurring sugars in fruit, vegetables...," says Rachel K. Johnson, PhD, professor of nutrition at the University of Vermont in Burlington. "As sweet as some of these things may taste, they contain relatively small amounts of sugar. Plus, nature's packaging comes with essential vitamins and minerals, along with water and fiber that slow the release of sugars into the bloodstream and prevent insulin spikes. (24)

What about the rest of your diet, your foods? Beware the additives, and especially the high fructose corn syrup.

As Dr. Mercola says, "**You simply MUST understand that because HFCS is so darn cheap, it is added to virtually every processed food.** Even if you consumed no soda or fruit, it is

very easy to exceed 25 grams of hidden fructose in your diet."
(25)

NO SUGAR AT ALL?

My husband asked, "Do you mean we should eat no sugar at all?"

A smaller amount of sugar, like we consumed in years past (including from natural fruits and healthy alternatives), could be part of a balanced diet. But because sugar has been added to so many foods, including the cheap and deadly high fructose corn syrup, because many of us want more and more sugar, and many consume soft drinks with high amounts, sugar levels are completely out of whack.

Until we can reduce the amount we eat and break the cravings or addictions, there is no hope to tackle the problem.

And watch out for juices, which you may think are healthy even if they don't include sweeteners. Why? Orange juice, as an example, contains 1.8 grams of fructose per ounce, the same as a can of soda. Eat the fruit instead.

The approach I am proposing in this book is to **reduce the cravings and break the addiction, get the body back in sync, lose weight and become more aware with a fresh start.** Bring down sugar consumption and use healthy alternatives (discussed in Chapter 4). So...

ARE YOU READY TO BREAK THE ADDICTION? ARE YOU READY TO LEARN ABOUT A NATURAL WAY TO DO THIS?

CHAPTER 2
HOW DO I BREAK THE ADDICTION, CURB THE CRAVINGS AND FEEL FULL?

In Chapter 1, we have established WHY sugar, at least too much of it, is very bad for you. Why would you be motivated to take action or want to curb your cravings or break your addiction unless you understand WHAT sugar is doing to you?

So now let's discuss the natural method of breaking the addiction or cravings, proven to help and to work. This chapter will discuss what it is, clinical tests that show it works and what's behind it. The next chapter will give you the actual action plan.

What is the natural method to help you?

It's Inhaling Specific Essential Oils!

What?

Yes, it is a proven and natural way to break sugar addiction and lose weight. **It works directly with your brain center**, quelling cravings and addiction, and helping you to feel satiated.

You see, aromatherapy (AROMAtherapy) is all about inhaling powerful and precious essential oil scents, the life force of plants which have different powers depending on the plant. They take action in the brain first and foremost.

Sugar addiction – addictions like to crack, heroin, nicotine, etc. – is controlled and handled in your brain.

The brain is your body's CONTROL CENTER! A portion of your brain is where your addiction is centered - it controls your pangs, cravings, addictions.

Your sense of smell is the ONLY sense tied directly to the limbic system of your brain.

Inhaling specific essential oils in a specific way will send instructions to your brain that you are not hungry, or that will give you satiety, or will help make you feel satisfied and that you got your natural rush and don't need the sugar.

Just like food, essential oils act to trigger responses in the body, such as suppression of sweet and food cravings, or feeling satisfied.

Essential oils are an easy, natural alternative to potentially solving the problem.

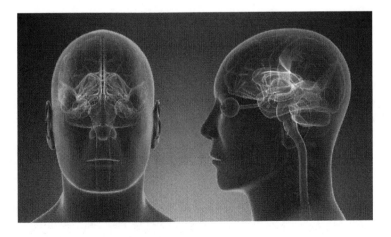

Here's a Summary of Five Studies Using Essential Oils & Scents for This Purpose

1) **Dr. Alan Hirsch, a neurologist who founded the Smell & Taste Treatment & Research Foundation** (1), conducted a test with more than 3,500 subjects.

He had the subjects inhale specific essential oils and scents to deprogram overweight people who ate lots of sugar and also overate. Over a period of 6 months, the participants lost an average of 5 pounds per month and were able to reprogram eating habits.

2) **Bryan Raudenbush , a professor of psychology at Wheeling Jesuit University** (2) in West Virginia, had a test group of 40 people inhale peppermint essential oil every 2 hours for five days. The next five days he gave them a placebo to inhale. During the week they inhaled peppermint, they consumed 1,800 fewer calories.

3) **A later study at Wheeling Jesuit, this time led by J.A. Reed** (along with Bryan Raudenbush, J. Alameida and B. Wershing) revealed that using peppermint essential oil reduced hunger levels and acted as an appetite suppressant. It evaluated hunger levels with and without inhalation. Participants rated their hunger levels and kept a food diary. Use of peppermint essential oil significantly reduced caloric intake and decreased cravings.

4) **The Human Neuro-Sensory Laboratory in Washington D.C.** discovered that people who inhaled specific essential oils

before meals **lost an average of 19 pounds in six months,** while the placebo group lost only 4 pounds.

5) **K.G. Stiles, an aromatherapy consultant** and holistic health coach, conducted a six week research study with six women. Any form of dieting was forbidden – they were to inhale essential oils but continue in their normal schedule. All six women lost weight. **Five of them lost 6-10 pounds.** (3)

6) In an animal study at **Osaka University** in Japan, rats were exposed to pink grapefruit oil for 15 minute intervals three times per week. It reduced their appetite and they lost weight. (3bis)

Let's look closer at the very large study by Dr. Hirsch.

DR. HIRSCH

The neurologist, Dr. Alan Hirsch, of the Smell & Taste Treatment & Research Foundation in Chicago clearly demonstrated in his large study specific essential oils and scents could deprogram overweight people whose normal response to the smell of rich, sugary foods like cakes, chocolate and doughnuts was to become hungry and overeat – that is, craving or addiction.

His test showed that inhaling throughout the day, and whenever they experienced a craving, simply inhibited the desire to eat, or controlled cravings or curbed appetite and provided satiety.

He also discovered that the more people used scent to control their appetite, the more weight they lost. When the brain signals being full or a sense of being satisfied, the craving stop, and we eat less. This mechanism can be triggered by the sense of smell.

Hirsch has written more than 100 articles on the psychological power of scent and conducted more than 180 studies on the senses of smell and taste, and various disorders and diseases. **The sense of smell has a profound effect on feelings of hunger and eating as well as emotions.**

In his previous research, Dr. Hirsch found that people preferred sweet smells, and that strongly sweet scents such as chocolate often triggered feelings of hunger and led to overeating or binge eating, while "neutral" sweet smells – like peppermint - actually curbed appetite. He also found that alternating scents was part of the success.

After six months, he found that, on average, the participants in his study lost five pounds a month. However he also found that those who did not lose weight either showed poor olfactory abilities or inhaled less than recommended and tended to snack more than five times a day.

In a New York Times article, Dr. Hirsch said, "A large part of the reason that you feel full is your brain interpreting that you've smelled it and tasted it," said Dr. Hirsch, a neurologist, psychiatrist and the founder of the Smell and Taste Treatment and Research Foundation in Chicago. (4)

In his study Dr. Hirsch stressed the fact that the aroma should be sniffed three times into each nostril and that the aroma should be sniffed as often as necessary. The results showed that those who inhaled often during the day were far more successful. Those who sniffed once or twice a day and expected the results to last all day were not as successful. (*I will comment on this, regarding bioavailability, later in the chapter.*) He also discovered that the subjects should alternate essential oil scents, using a minimum of three.

EMOTIONAL EATING

Emotional states can trigger desire for food. Emotional food cravings can be controlled and the feelings by inhaling certain essential oils. The sense of smell helps increase or decrease appetite and calms irrational emotional responses to food. The sense of smell can give us control instead of depending solely on our will power.

WHAT DO WE DRAW FROM THESE TESTS FOR OUR OWN APPLICATION?

1) The most important piece of information found in the study was to inhale often at first, plus every time a craving presented itself.

2) The essential oils should be alternated to avoid desensitization and help with success.

3) Dr. Hirsch had his patients inhale <u>3 times in each nostril</u>.

WHAT ESSENTIAL OILS ARE PREFERRED FOR WEIGHT LOSS AND SUGAR ADDICTION? WHICH WERE USED IN VARIOUS TESTS OR HAVE THE PROPERTIES NEEDED?

Alternate

Two of the top essential oils sited by various experts are Grapefruit and Peppermint. Here is a list of preferred essential oils.

Peppermint Essential Oil

Pink Grapefruit Essential Oil

Lemon Essential Oil

Sweet Orange Essential Oil

Bergamot Essential Oil

Ylang Ylang Essential Oil

Cinnamon and Clove Essential Oils

Lime Essential Oil

Fennel Essential Oil

Dr. Hirsch found that **PEPPERMINT specifically helped highly with the SATIETY function** – excellent to use so you do not overeat, or if you have persistent cravings. (5)

SUMMARY OF THE TOP ESSENTIAL OILS FOR SUGAR ADDICTION & WEIGHT LOSS

Note that I explain aromatherapy and use of essential oils later in this chapter, if it is a new subject to you!

Peppermint: Peppermint provides unique weight loss benefits. Peppermint is also a digestive aid and helps with digestive problems and tummy aches. In aromatherapy, the qualities are clearing of energy, uplifting of the mind, reducing fatigue, refreshes, and stimulates. It's an anti-inflammatory, anti-bacterial and anti-spasmodic.

Pink Grapefruit: A natural weight loss appetite suppressant. In the body it can help dissolve fat by a process called lipolysis, and it's an immune-stimulant. In aromatherapy, it is uplifting & cleansing, reduces tension and helps lift happiness. It can also prevent bloating, water retention and help dissolve fat.

Bergamot: This little-known and pleasant citrus stimulates the endocrine system and thereby increases metabolism. It also creates calm and feelings of well-being. In aromatherapy, it is relaxing, restorative, calming and emotionally supportive. It can also help with insomnia.

Sweet Orange: Helps overcome depression and has a calming impact on the nervous system. It helps with liver support and is also an immune-stimulant. In aromatherapy, it unblocks bad energy, helps circulation, and calms an overwhelmed mind while reducing pessimism.

Ylang Ylang: Assists feeling of well and calm, it can reduce impulses. It has a harmonizing effect on the heart (known to slow a rapid heartbeat) and bring down blood pressure. It's an aphrodisiac, and in aromatherapy encourages euphoria, helps one to experience joy and promotes sensuality.

Cinnamon: Cinnamon can help support healthy insulin sensitivity in the brain and support the proper rate of blood glucose.

Clove Bud: helps metabolism and stimulated digestion. It's also an immune-stimulant and anti-inflammatory. Clove bud essential oil is a traditional remedy for a myriad of digestive dysfunctions. In aromatherapy, it warms the mind and body, improves confidence.

Fennel: In ancient Greece, Rome and into the Middle Ages, fennel seeds were eaten to suppress the appetite. Soldiers used it when food stores were low. An 8 week scientific study with fennel aromatherapy and rats reduced calories consumed and faster digestion. They were exposed twice per day for 10 minutes over 8 weeks.

ESSENTIAL OILS FOR EMOTIONAL EATING? WHAT ABOUT STRESS?

Essential oils can help here as well. A whole host of emotional issues could trigger eating. Choose scents that resonate with you, including **Lemongrass, Frankincense, May Chang, Rose Geranium, Neroli, Rosemary and Palmarosa.**

Unfortunately, most of us experience more stress than we should these days. The mechanics behind stress can actually trigger hunger and eating as well. Cortisol kicks in when you are stressed, your blood pressure rises. It initially was used by the human body to help keep up alive against, for instance, animal attacks or mortal dangers. Today, a startling thing like almost being in a car accident will cause a rush of stress and cortisol.

But unfortunately, far too many things are not life-threatening but cause stress: a bad boss, a sick family member, not making enough money to meet obligations, a bully in the neighborhood, a bad marriage, bad traffic when you are late, etc. And these things can be constant.

Cortisol floods in, which can initially dampen hunger. Once the stress dies down, hunger hormones build up telling the body to refuel. This can lead to cravings, hunger pangs or binge eating... and poor sleep. Without enough sleep, hormones are also whacky and can cause poor eating habits and sugar binges.

The Mayo Clinic says, "The long-term activation of the stress-response system — and the subsequent overexposure to cortisol and other stress hormones — can disrupt almost all your body's processes. This puts you at increased risk of numerous health problems..." (6)

There are essential oils which excel at stress reduction and if stress is a mainstay in your life, you might consider adding this to your arsenal to help with emotional eating or binges.

Some of the best essential oils for stress are Lavender, Rosemary, Frankincense, Rose Geranium, Ylang Ylang, Neroli, Bergamot and blends like Zen De-Stress (which contains Lavender, Clary Sage, Neroli, Roman Chamomile & Rosemary) is one of our most popular along with Zen Bliss.

THE POWER OF AROMATHERAPY – WHAT'S IT ALL ABOUT?

For those of you whom are not familiar with aromatherapy and essential oils, this is a short summary. (You can also refer to my book, "Essential Oils Have Super Powers: From Solving Everyday Wellness Problems to Taking on Superbugs".)

Aromatherapy is the use of essential oils for psychological and physical well-being. The father of modern aromatherapy, Rene-Maurice Gattefossé, coined the term, but aromatherapy dates back thousands and thousands of years.

If you love reading trivia, fun facts and historical information, pick up my short book on the history of essential oils and aromatic plants.

 Aromatherapy treats our emotional, physical and spiritual health.

Essential oils are sometimes called the "life force" of a plant, an aromatic substance extracted from plants that has hundreds of compounds that can help us. Essential oils are almost always anti-bacterial, but depending on the plant and its makeup, holds different powers (like reducing inflammation, uplift, reducing stress, improving memory, help with sleep, etc.)

Aromatherapy can be used for **medical applications** (such as healing a burn or wound, for anti-bacterial applications, bringing down inflammation, attacking bacteria, help a chemotherapy patient with nausea, etc.)

Aromatherapy can be used for **wellness applications** (helping one to sleep restfully, calming an anxiety attack, helping one focus, helping with grief, improving the immune system, in a therapeutic massage, etc.)

Aromatherapy can be used for "**environmental atmosphere**" (such as diffusing scents to create an inviting, grounded or energetic room; calm patients in a dentist-office, as well as purifying the air of microbes.)

They can be used **proactively and for preventative care** (disinfecting the air of bacteria, helping to relax for sleep, supporting the immune system), but also for <u>active care</u> (like disinfecting a wound, clearing congestion or reducing a headache.)

The bottom line is that essential oils can penetrate not only the blood-brain barrier, but they can also penetrate the skin, follow nerve pathways, follow the meridians, and provide healing and balance even at the cellular level such as cellular memory and limbic system (that emotional control center.) This includes helping to break sugar addiction or helping you to feel full.

While aromatherapy has been recognized around the world for centuries and used in many countries today, it is only recently that they are becoming more known in the U.S. They are not taught in medical schools. However, even the most famous of U.S. hospitals are starting to offer aromatherapy for pain and sleep aids.

There is a growing body of clinical and scientific studies in the U.S. to prove what centuries of knowledge and other countries have told us – essential oils hold amazing powers.

They are almost all antibacterial and can disinfect and even kill superbugs. They help with mood, bringing down stress, helping with memory or focus, uplifting, help with sleep and more. Each essential oil has different compounds that can help with different issues.

The HIGHEST AND BEST USE of essential oils is by inhaling them, because they go immediately to the limbic system in the brain, our dashboard, and instruct the body what to do.

In some cases, using them topical ALWAYS MIXED IN A CARRIER OIL (because they are very concentrated and powerful) can help with inflammation, tummy aches, burns & wounds, headaches, congestion and more.

BIOAVAILABILITY IS IMPORTANT TO UNDERSTAND

Remember in Dr. Hirsch's tests, he found that people who only inhaled a few times per day were not as successful? This is because of bioavailability. I promised to explain this.

Bioavailability is the proportion of a substance introduced into the body able to have an active effect.

When inhaled, essential oils have about a 70% bioavailability. Compare this to an oral drug like morphine, with a 23.9% bioavailability – likewise for anything swallowed that goes through the stomach, liver & kidneys and is broken down by various acids.

 The amount of time an essential oil stays active when inhaled (peak concession) is 20 minutes – the time it has reached its effectiveness peak.

This is why you are going to inhale every 2 hours at the beginning, and whenever you experience a craving.

Now, topical peak concession is 360 minutes! It lasts longer but its availability is only about 7%. For something like inflammation or indigestion, it is good that the effectiveness peak is stretching out – but the bioavailability is lower.

This is why highest and best use is typically inhaling essential oils!

I explain this in one of my Essential Oil Zen podcasts here.

Aromatherapy is a deep and useful science and art, so helpful for mind and body. Use of essential oils in this case, for sugar cravings, breaking addiction, helping with weight loss, stimulating your immune system, and helping with emotional eating is a natural way to work directly with your brain, hormones and body.

IF YOU WANT TO UNDERSTAND MORE OF THE SCIENCE BEHIND ADDICTION, READ ON. IF NOT, PROCEED TO CHAPTER 3!

What is involved physically in your brain when you are addicted to sugar (or any other substance)? Your Nucleus Accumbens releases the dopamine. It's a group of neuons located mid brain. These neurons then connect to a variety of places within the limbic system.

The release of dopamine (and serotonin) in the nucleus accumbens creates feelings of pleasure. When you eat sugar, or crave sugar, you are lighting up the nucleus accumbens with a surge of electrochemical activity – which is the same pathways that regulate our food and water-seeking behavior.

By directly or indirectly influencing the molecules of pleasure, sugar or desire for sugar triggers key neurochemical events that are central to our feelings of both reward and disappointment.

Dopamine is also the key molecule involved in the memory of pleasurable acts. Dopamine is part of the reason why we remember how much we liked the sugar we consumed (or the high we experienced.) The nucleus accumbens is involved in modulating the emotional strength of the signals.

Hunger for sugar, nicotine or drugs in abstinent addicts is not all in the head, or strictly psychological. Craving has a biological basis.

Finding a way to override the dopamine-mediated mid-brain commands is the essential key to recovery from addiction. And this is why inhaling essential oils, which goes directly to the limbic system, which is natural, and which can create the feeling of pleasure and satiation is exciting! (7)

When the end result is better or improved health, loss of weight and control of eating habits, it's a win-win.

CHAPTER 3
ACTION PLAN – WHAT TO DO

*"Let food be thy medicine
and medicine be thy food." -Hippocrates*

Let's beat the cravings and get on a great path.

GET YOUR TOOLS READY

1] Get <u>at least 3 essential oils</u> (per Dr. Hirsch's recommendation of alternating scents). We recommend **Peppermint** and **Pink Grapefruit**, the 2 top essential oils for weight loss and addiction. Make sure they are therapeutic-grade. The third or additional essential oils can depend on your likes (flowery or citrus). **Zen Air Bliss** may be a good choice as it is a pure blend that mixes flowery and citrus: **ylang ylang, bergamot, sweet orange, neroli** (orange blossoms).

You might also consider **Bergamot, Sweet Orange** or **Lemon** (citrus), if you like citrus scents. Or **Cinnamon and/or Clove** (I especially like Clove), strong, spicy, non-citrus scents that are known to help with weight reduction and appetite control.

* <u>Our link at the beginning of this book gets you a free therapeutic-grade full size peppermint when you buy any other essential oil or oils at 50% off, including grapefruit</u> (quantities go fast.)

II. <u>You can inhale directly from the bottle</u> as often as you wish and need. However, you must be sure to <u>tightly cap</u> the bottle and keep it in a darker, cooler place. If you are on the go, you should get one of the tools below.

Inhalers. Put your essential oil inside and simply open it to breathe in when needed. We have some and you can find them on Amazon.

Aromatherapy bracelet or necklace. Put several drops of you oil on the lava stone of the bracelet, or filler of the necklace, and pull it to your nose whenever you need to inhale during the day (and every 2 hours).

Diffuser. Diffuse the essential oil in your home, office or room so you inhale it constantly. This might be good for the beginning of your journey, and at night if you tend to get "night cravings" and want to raid the fridge at midnight. Lavender would be a good one to use for sleep.

Simple cotton ball or tissue. Not as effective (evaporation will come into play faster) but you can put a drop or two on and use it at your nose.

ACTION PLAN

I. FOR THE FIRST 2 WEEKS, INHALE EVERY 2 HOURS.

Following Dr. Hirsch's recommendation, inhale 3 times into each nostril, taking nice deep breaths.

II. INHALE WHENEVER YOU GET A SUGAR CRAVING

III. INHALE BEFORE EACH MEAL (it will help you feel full – and as the fructose and sugar detox from your system, your satiety functions will eventually return.)

Note: It may helpful to keep a journal during this time – of when you inhaled, which essential oil you used, and times when cravings hit.

If you tend to get night cravings and have had a habit of getting out of bed to raid the fridge or eat something, you could DIFFUSE LAVENDER in your bedroom at night. Lavender is known to be the best for sleep (deep sleep) and relaxation. I don't recommend using Peppermint at night as it could keep you awake! Otherwise, keep your inhaler under your pillow and use it!

IV. ALTERNATE EACH DAY OR HALF DAY WITH DIFFERENT ESSENTIAL OILS. Dr. Hirsch said this will help with any desensitization issues.

V. STARTING IN WEEK 3, INHALE EVERY 4 HOURS AND WHENEVER A SUGAR CRAVING HITS. IF YOU ARE STILL EXPERIENCING A LOT OF CRAVINGS, THEN GO BACK TO EVERY 2 HOURS FOR ANOTHER WEEK. IF NOT, YOU CAN SLOWLY WEAN DOWN.

VI. ALSO BE SURE TO TAKE YOUR ESSENTIAL OILS OR INHALER WITH YOU, AND USE IT:

✓ When you go food shopping (inhale before you go into the grocery store, and again inside if you need to.)
✓ When you dine out (inhale before you go into the restaurant)

- ✓ At games, concerts, parties or events you might attend that have food and soda or sugary soft drinks you want to avoid.
- ✓ Any time you feel urge to snack or take second helpings

THREE KEYS FOR RESULTS:

1. **REPETITION!** Keep up your use of essential oils! Dr. Hirsch found that the subjects who kept up the plan and inhaled often lost the weight and succeeded. Be sure to inhale 3 times into each nostril (that is 6 times total).

2. **CONSISTENCY.** Use your essential oils every two hours in the first two weeks, and then every four or five hours in the next week if your sugar cravings are slowing down or going away. Be consistent. Set an alarm if you need to, or keep that journal. The more you are consistent and help your body help itself, the more successful you will be.

3. **TAKE THIS TIME TO REVIEW YOUR LIFESTYLE HABITS.** You will be weaning yourself of sugar cravings and overeating, and you will start to lose weight. But you need to be sure your portion controls of what eat are good; examine whether you eat processed or fast foods, and take this time to eliminate or slow down on it (if that is what you have been eating); bump up vegetables, whole grains and good proteins – or review what kind of diet you should be on and try it.

Be sure to drink lots of fresh water (and avoid juices, soft drinks and such); get good sleep and rest; get exercise and some daily time outside in the fresh air.

If you don't exercise much – then start daily walks, or morning yoga or tai chi before work or school, or biking or swimming. Try BFS for high impact short-time available workouts.

Visualize what you would like to look like in a month, six months and a year.

As you start to lose weight, maybe you will get a new haircut or freshen up how you look, start some new healthy habits and journey.

Don't beat yourself up if you have a set-back. Just start again and keep it up. Know you can do it!

If it helps, spend 5-10 minutes in the morning, quietly meditating and thinking about the day ahead and how you are beating sugar and changing your life. Use this quiet time to gain strength.

Cutting down on sugar and even eliminating it is going to help change your body and its tastes. Use the time to look at everything and get a fresh start!

Be sure to download the essential oil SAFETY TIPS information at the front of the book.

CHAPTER 4

THE GOAL OF A HEALTHY LIFESTYLE, GAINING CONTROL + SUGAR SUBSTITUTES

"Diet is about pounds, exercise is about inches.
Diet is about weight, exercise is about health."
—Dr. Robert Lustig

K.G. Stiles shared two helpful nuggets about dieting in a recent NAHA (National Association for Holistic Aromatherapy) seminar (1).

1) In a dieting / no dieting study of more than 2,000 sets of twins from Finland, age 16 - 25, results showed that the dieting – "weight loss plan" twins were 2 - 3 times more likely to become overweight, as compared to their non-dieting twins.

2) Study and after study shows that, "it is now well established that the more people engage in dieting, the more they gain weight in the long-term," says Stiles.

Try to approach eating as something that you do to enjoy and to nourish your strong body. **Think of good healthy food as your friend, and "empty addictive" food as not having a place in your body.** Investigate what balance of foods and portions will satisfy you.

There are many ideas and good themes out there, from blood type affinity, to your ayurvedic body type and foods, to the various plans like paleo.

 Be aware of what you eat and buy, and look at the wrappers. Any substance that ends in –ose is going to be a sugar, and you will be shocked to see that everything from pretzels and mustard to processed meats may have sugar. Please watch out for sugary morning cereals! Please don't drink soda.

Do I personally hate sugar? My husband asked me this! No! A little sugar might be part of the overall balance and "spice of life", and if we consumed the small amounts we did 100 years ago – then it's OK. We should try to consume no more than 4 teaspoons per day. In today's world, that might sound insane. A small dark chocolate after a meal, some sugar in your coffee or tea, a cookie now and then. No sodas.

The problem is because sugar is addictive, it is sometimes hard to "eat just one". Because sugar is "empty", it can deplete our own body stores. And lots of sugar causes illness. High fructose corn syrup is added to everything, and most of us are already past our normal intake limit. Don't forget, HFCS stops our satiety controls and puts strain on the liver. Refer back to those facts in Chapter 1.

So for most people, the best approach is to break the sugar addiction and stop the cravings, and then try to proceed (with the help of essential oils) eating very little of it – and start to use alternatives while adopting a good diet!

ALTERNATES TO SUGAR?

There are substitutes for sugar which are healthier. Consider the following – but no more than a few teaspoons per day please.

Here is an important point about these suggestions. Dr. Axe says that these natural sweeteners "… are lower on the glycemic index than sugar. Where regular table sugar scores 100, many of these sweeteners score closer to a 50, so half the glycemic index. That means they affect your body in a lesser amount to where they're not going to cause your energy levels to drop or increase or spike your insulin levels, increasing your risk of diabetes, like a lot of the other sugars out there today." (2)

✳ **RAW HONEY.** Look for "raw" on the label, and look for a darker honey, which means more antioxidants. This kind will be the healthiest for you. Honey itself has many great wellness qualities. If you suffer from seasonal allergies, buy LOCAL honey because the bees pollinate locally and this can help you adapt to local pollen!

Honey is very healing in its own right, and has anti-bacterial qualities. In addition, it is similar to glucose and is very easy for the body to digest.

NOTE: A Texas A&M university study shows that 76% of grocery-store honeys contained NO pollen. Go for local and organic. (3)

* **STEVIA.** Stevia is a no-calorie, all-natural sweetener that comes from the leaf of a flowering plant. But avoid processed stevia (that darned processed stuff again.) Stevia is especially good if you have high blood sugar or are very overweight.

* **RAISINS.** I love to sprinkle a few raisins with my walnuts & almonds, or put some in yogurt or in a salad. My mom used to give me those little red boxes of raisins as a snack when I was a toddler!

* **REAL MAPLE SYRUP.** Go for 100 percent pure organic maple syrup. Look for grade B or even grade C that is USDA-certified organic – **not processed stuff (or pancake syrup) that has sugar additives or high fructose corn syrup!** Pure maple syrup has 54 antioxidant compounds. Our early American ancestors used maple syrup as one of the main sweeteners, and it stands today!

  Real maple syrup has calcium and zinc and a significant amount of riboflavin, too.

* **MOLASSES.** Molasses is what's left over during the process of refining of sugar cane into white sugar! Molasses is perhaps the most nutrient rich of all sweeteners, providing a significant amount of calcium, iron, magnesium, potassium and vitamin B6.

MOVE YOUR BODY – EXERCISE!

If you are overweight and taken down by sugar, you might not be exercising, have no energy or feel sick. Exercise alone will not help you lose weight BUT it will help you build muscle, tone, generate endorphins, feel good and feel inspired. Exercise WILL improve your insulin sensitivity and lower insulin levels.

You don't have to go crazy at first, if you have not been exercising at all. Even 15 minutes per day can help you.

Did you know that exercise can help with disease prevention? I love this study: Tawain looked at the death rates of 400,000 people, and found that just 15 minutes of exercise per day could increase life span by as much as three years, even for those with heart disease. (4) An American study of 38,000 men showed that physical activity and exercise were more important in preventing heart disease than normal weight. (5)

Whether adding walking to your everyday schedule, or calisthenics, or joining a gym or spin class, trying the new BFR approach, or perhaps yoga or tai chi, workouts with the Wii, biking or swimming, find what you can do and what you WANT to do – and do it. When you enjoy and want to do the activity, it will be easy for you.

YOU CAN DO THIS!

YOUR MINDSET MUST BE NOT ONE OF SUGAR DEPRIVATION – BUT OF SUGAR REDUCTION AND THE BEAUTY OF YOUR HEALTH AND BODY ON THE OTHER SIDE!

REFERENCE: TYPES OF SUGAR

Glucose: This is the sugar that is in our bloodstream, every cell uses it and it is burned up. But fructose & high fructose corn syrup has been replaced in the U.S. as a main sugar source.

Sucrose: the common table sugar. It is part glucose and part fructose. Most sugar is refined, stripped of all nutrients and "empty calories".

Fructose: A natural sugar found in fruits, usually combined with fiber, vitamins and nutrients. However, when fructose is processed and used alone or in HFCS, it is metabolized in the liver, and causes all sorts of issues including disrupting satiety controls.

HFCS (High fructose corn syrup): completely derived from cornstarch, composed of fructose and glucose. It is cheap and used heavily in the U.S.

ACKNOWLEDGEMENTS

The great writings and research of Gary Taubes and his book "The Case Against Sugar" have been influential to me, as is Dr. Robert Lustig and his work, including "Fat Chance". I admire Dr. Mercola tremendously and encourage you to read his latest work, "Fat for Fuel".

I thank the great fellow authors in the mastermind groups as well as the leaders including Chandler Bolt, Sean Sumners, and Tom Corson-Knowles.

And I always thank my fantastic husband, Harlan, for all of his support and being the perfect "sounding board".

ABOUT THE AUTHOR

Kathy Heshelow is an Amazon best-selling author, and has written a number of books over the years, with a focus in the wellness and beauty domain *(and some in the passive-income real estate world.)*

She actually learned many of the wellness skills and concepts when she lived in Paris, France for 16 years (such as Skin Brushing, Essential Oils for wellness, European skin care techniques.) This has prompted her to start the Sublime Wellness Lifestyle Series of eBooks in March 2017. She is founder of Sublime Beauty and Sublime Naturals.

Follow her new podcast on iTunes, "Essential Oil Zen".

Heshelow lives in Florida with her husband and 4 legged family. She can be reached at Kathy@sb-naturals.com or through www.kathyheshelow.com

REFERENCES

Who Is This Book For?

(1) Why Diets Don't Work, by Meg Selig. Psychology Today. https://www.psychologytoday.com/blog/changepower/2010 10/why-diets-dont-workand-what-does

CHAPTER 1

1) The Harmful Effects of Sugar on Mind and Body. http://rense.com/general45/sguar.htm

2) Mercola, Dr. Joseph. Fructose. This Addictive Commonly Used Food Feeds Cancer Cells, Triggers Weight Gain, and Promotes Premature Aging http://articles.mercola.com/sites/articles/archive/2010/04/2 0/sugar-dangers.aspx#_edn1

3) Taubes, Gary. The Case Against Sugar. Alfred Knopf, NY. 2016.

4) VisionGain. https://www.visiongain.com/Press_Release/405/Diabetes-drugs-market-will-reach-55-3bn-in-2017-with-further-growth-to-2023-predicts-visiongain-in-new-report

5) The Harmful Effects Of Sugar On Mind And Body. Macrobiotics.co.uk http://rense.com/general45/sugar.htm

6) Reuben, Dr. David. "Everything You Always Wanted to Know About Nutrition."

(7) The American Journal of Clinical Nutrition . "Consumption of High-Fructose Corn Syrup in Beverages May Play a Role in the Epidemic of Obesity" by George A Bray, Samara Joy Nielsen, and Barry M Popkin.

(8) The Harmful Effects Of Sugar On Mind And Body. Macrobiotics.co.uk http://rense.com/general45/sugar.htm

(9) Taubes, Gary. The Case Against Sugar. Alfred Knopf, NY. 2016.

(10) Insulin and Cancer.
https://www.ncbi.nlm.nih.gov/pubmed/14713323

(11) Taubes, Gary. The Case Against Sugar. Alfred Knopf, NY. 2016.

(12) Ji, Sayer. GreenMedInfo. Research Reveals How Sugar Causes Cancer. Aug 30th, 2014.
http://www.greenmedinfo.com/blog/research-reveals-how-sugar-causes-cancer

(13) Dr. Richard Jacoby and Raquel Baldelomar. Sugar Crush: How to Reduce Inflammation, Reverse Nerve Damage and Reclaim Good Health. Harper Collins. 2015.

(14) Taubes, Gary. The Case Against Sugar. Alfred Knopf, NY. 2016.

(15) Taubes, Gary. The Case Against Sugar. Alfred Knopf, NY. 2016.

(16) IBID

(17) "Sugar, not fat, exposed as deadly villain in obesity epidemic." The Guardian. https://www.theguardian.com/society/2013/mar/20/sugar-deadly-obesity-epidemic

(18) Dr. Richard Jacoby and Raquel Baldelomar. Sugar Crush: How to Reduce Inflammation, Reverse Nerve Damage and Reclaim Good Health. Harper Collins. 2015.

(19) Evidence for sugar addiction: Behavioral and neurochemical effects of intermittent, excessive sugar intake. Nicole M. Avena, Pedro Rada, Bartley G. Hoebel. on Science Direct. http://www.sciencedirect.com/science/article/pii/S0149763407000589

(20) "Experts Agree: Sugar Might Be as Addictive as Cocaine", Written by Anna Schaefer and Kareem Yasin. Medically Reviewed by Peggy Pletcher, MS, RD, LD, CDE on October 10, 2016. Healthline. http://www.healthline.com/health/food-nutrition/experts-is-sugar-addictive-drug

(21) Taubes, Gary. The Case Against Sugar. Alfred Knopf, NY. 2016.

(22) "Experts Agree: Sugar Might Be as Addictive as Cocaine", Written by Anna Schaefer and Kareem Yasin. Medically Reviewed by Peggy Pletcher, MS, RD, LD, CDE on October 10, 2016. Healthline. http://www.healthline.com/health/food-nutrition/experts-is-sugar-addictive-drug

(23) Taubes, Gary. The Case Against Sugar. Alfred Knopf, NY. 2016.

(24) Is Sugar Really That Bad for You?
http://www.health.com/health/article/0,,20637702,00.html

(25) Mercola, Dr. Joseph. Fructose: This Addictive Commonly Used Food Feeds Cancer Cells, Triggers Weight Gain, and Promotes Premature Aging.
http://articles.mercola.com/sites/articles/archive/2010/04/20/sugar-dangers.aspx

CHAPTER 2

(1) http://www.smellandtaste.org/

(2)
http://www.wju.edu/about/adm_news_story.asp?iNewsID=1106

(3) Feb 2017 NAHA webinar conference. Using Aromatherapy for Weight Loss Support with KG Stiles. NAHA members only. K.G. Stiles, BA, CBT, CBP, LMT is a metaphysician, holistic health coach and aromatherapy consultant providing expert essential oil services since 1980.

(3bis) Jiao Shena, Akira Niijimab, Mamoru Tanidaa, Yuko Horiia, Keiko Maedaa, Katsuya Nagaia. Institute for Protein Research, Osaka University, Japan. 2004-2005.
http://www.sciencedirect.com/science/article/pii/S0304394005001084

(4) New York Times. "A Slimmer You May Be a Whiff Away". by Abby Ellin. http://www.nytimes.com/2009/06/18/fashion/18skin.html

(5) https://aromaoiltherapynu.wordpress.com/tag/dr-hirsch/

(6) Mayo Clinic. http://www.mayoclinic.org/healthy-lifestyle/stress-management/in-depth/stress/art-20046037

(7) Adapted from the Chemical Carousel: What Science Tells Us About Beating Addiction by Dirk Hanson © 2008. http://addiction-dirkh.blogspot.com/2010/02/nucleus-accumbens.html

CHAPTER 4

(1) Feb 2017 NAHA webinar conference. Using Aromatherapy for Weight Loss Support with KG Stiles. NAHA members only. K.G. Stiles, BA, CBT, CBP, LMT is a metaphysician, holistic health coach and aromatherapy consultant providing expert essential oil services since 1980.

(2) Axe, Dr. Josh. The 5 Best Sugar Substitutes. https://draxe.com/sugar-substitutes/

(3) Food Safety News. Tests Show Most Store Honey Isn't Honey, by Andrew Schneider. http://www.foodsafetynews.com/2011/11/tests-show-most-store-honey-isnt-honey/#.WQNrb9y1v3h

(4) C.P. Wen et al. "Minimum Amount of Physical Activity for Reduced Mortality and Extended Life Expectancy: A Prospective Cohort Study." Lancet 378 (2011).

(5) J.A. Mitchell et al. "The Impact of Combined Health Factors on Cardiovascular Disease Mortality." American Health Journal 160 (2010)

FDA Disclaimer

This book and information is for reference and education, and represents my views and research, including the research, publications and clinical tests of others. Essential oils and aromatherapy, for me, support what the body needs and requires to thrive, and they work at the holistic level of mind-body-spirit.

I fully stand behind the natural wellness properties of essential oils, using them in my daily life.

However, the statements in this book are not intended as a substitute for professional healthcare nor meant to diagnose, cure or prevent medical conditions or serious disease.

Every illness or injury requires supervision by a medical doctor, integrative doctor and/or an alternative medicine practitioner such as a certified holistic doctor or certified aromatherapist practitioner.

Books by Heshelow

Essential Oils Have Super Powers®: From Solving Everyday Wellness Problems to Taking on Superbugs

Essential Oils Have Super Powers Series
#1 THE CRISIS OF ANTIBIOTIC-RESISTANT BACTERIA AND HOW ESSENTIAL OILS CAN HELP
#2 ANECDOTES, FUN FACTS & FASCINATING HISTORY OF ESSENTIAL OILS & AROMATIC PLANTS
#3 HOW ESSENTIAL OILS CAN HELP ME
#4 MIND-BODY-SPIRIT & AROMATHERAPY

Sublime Wellness Lifestyle Series
#1 Turmeric: How to Use It For YOUR Wellness
#2 Secrets to a Better Immune System: 3 Easy Steps
#3 Break Sugar Cravings or Addiction, Feel Full, Lose Weight

Phytoceramides: Anti Aging at its Best

GET FREE BOOKS & SECRET PROMOS FROM KATHY

I invite you to leave a review of this book, and share your thoughts & comments! Thank you! Kathy Heshelow